BOEING

GW01086160

ALAN J. WRIGHT

PLYMOUTH PRESS

IAN ALLAN
Publishing

Previous page:

Unlike many airlines, Kuwait's national flag carrier has not incorporated the country's colours into its livery, preferring the use of an attractive blue on the fuselage and fin. All four 747 combis are painted in this scheme which has the company's title displayed in both English and Arabic. Deliveries began in the summer of 1978, the third becoming 9K-ADC when arrived in the following February. Subsequently the type has maintained the long-haul sectors, although on some timings the 747s are to be found covering stages which are usually the responsibility of the wide-bodied twins.
Peter R. March

First published 1989 — *Boeing 747*
First published 1992 — *Boeing 757/767*
Combined edition 1998

ISBN — Ian Allan Publishing edition
    0 7110 2587 8
ISBN — Plymouth Press edition
    1 882663 24 1

Published by Ian Allan Publishing

an imprint of Ian Allan Publishing Ltd, Terminal House, Station Approach, Shepperton, Surrey TW17 8AS. Printed by Ian Allan Printing Ltd, Riverdene, Molesey Road, Hersham,

INTRODUCTION

Although a commonplace event, the sight of a fully-laden 747 on its take-off run never fails to give the impression that its progress is too leisurely to achieve an airborne state. Having disproved this, its climb away appears equally laborious – the aircraft apparently hanging in the sky, undecided on its future. Of course it is the sheer size of the airliner which provides these illusions for the onlooker; those within notice little difference from any other apart from the spacious cabin proportions. During the past 18 years or so, millions of passengers have flown in the mighty Boeing which certainly revolutionised air travel following its service entry in 1970.

It was as early as 1964 when the USAF initiated a design competition for a large cargo carrier, leading to development contracts being awarded to Boeing, Douglas and Lockheed. Much effort was expended by the three companies, but after extensive studies of the various proposals, Lockheed was given the task of producing the enormous transport which became the C-5A Galaxy. Boeing was naturally disappointed at the outcome, but the research work undertaken at government expense was not wasted. With market research indicating the need for an outsize civil airliner by the 1970s, the company turned its attention to this interesting challenge. Throughout the winter of 1965–66, a number of layouts were considered. Originally a fuselage with a 'double-bubble' cross-section was favoured, but this arrangement did not

attract much support from the numerous airlines consulted. Finally, it was a single-deck cabin which was selected with the now familiar 'hump' on top of the forward fuselage containing the flight deck and limited passenger accommodation.

Pan American played a large part in refining the Boeing design, eventually ordering 25 of the monsters on 13 April 1966, although the manufacturer waited until other carriers had committed themselves before giving the go-ahead for production on 25 July. Appropriately, the world's largest airliner required what was to become the world's largest building in terms of volume. A site some 30 miles (48 km) north of Seattle was earmarked for the new structure, which, after only six months, was at a sufficiently advanced stage for 747 work to begin in earnest. Everything associated with the design was large so it was not long before the media began to refer to it as a 'jumbo-sized' airliner. Although somewhat more graceful than an elephant, nonetheless the name was generally adopted until everyone knew of the 'jumbo-jet' even if they had never heard of a Boeing 747.

With such a daunting task, any delay in the completion of the first machine would have been understandable, but as forecast two years earlier the doors of the Everett building opened at 10.30 on 30 September 1968 to allow the 747 to make its debut. Preparations were then made for its maiden flight which of course was eagerly awaited. Originally it had

been expected to take place on 17 December – an appropriate date because it was the anniversary of the Wright brothers' epic flight at Kitty Hawk in 1903. This time the target was not achieved due to tests with the major on-board systems taking longer than anticipated plus the necessary extensive ground-running of the new turbofans. Final checks were made in late January 1969 when high speed taxying trials were satisfactorily completed. Only seven or so weeks behind schedule, the first of the new generation aircraft rolled majestically along the runway for some 4,500 ft (1,370 m) before lifting its 300-ton frame into the air on 9 February. Seventy-six minutes later it was successfully back on the ground for a few minor corrections to be incorporated before its second sortie six days later.

Supporting such an enormous weight called for a robust undercarriage. At an early stage the design utilised 16 main wheels shared equally amongst four bogie units positioned in line abreast, but this formation was changed before production. By moving the under-fuselage pair forward, space was provided for the outer legs to retract sideways and in so doing also ensure that the loads inflicted on airport runways was more evenly distributed. This weight had caused Boeing much trouble as construction proceeded because despite strenuous efforts it steadily increased. To maintain the promised range and payload performance a higher take-off weight was necessary – a requirement which brought new problems in its wake.

Naturally the powerplant had a considerable responsibility in ensuring that the 747 defied gravity, but the engines were also new and suffered their own development setbacks. Each demand for increased thrust brought more difficulties for Pratt & Whitney, but the company managed to develop an uprated specimen of the JT9D although it suffered more than its share of teething troubles before the modified engines settled down to give reliable service with the airlines later in 1970. Meanwhile, flight testing continued apace – the five aircraft dedicated to the task completing the programme and gaining the type's certificate of airworthiness at the end of 1969. During the year one of the batch made the 747's first intercontinental journey when it flew to Le Bourget on the occasion of the Paris Air Show. Visitors were much impressed by the standard of comfort shown in the fully furnished, 382-seat interior.

Back at the factory, 22 aircraft had been rolled-out by mid-October, but alarmingly 17 of these had no powerplant. Sub-contractors continued to manufacture components so it was very difficult to slow down assembly without causing still more headaches. Obviously deliveries were likely to be affected – a situation not to the liking of launch customer Pan Am because of the evaporation of any lead advantage over competitors. With two aircraft on strength the airline was able to prepare for the 747's first commercial service – an event which finally took place on 22 January 1970. It was not without incident, however, because earlier a 24-hour delay had been caused by engine trouble. Later, as the aircraft taxied out for its inaugural departure, an overheating JT9D forced a return to the terminal for another six-hour wait. A substitute machine finally made history when it left New York bound for London. The much-heralded age of the jumbo-jet had arrived.

By mid-year many of the major carriers had received their first deliveries. BOAC was one of this group although the airline had a problem of its own to overcome. A dispute between the corporation and it pilots had long been festering with the consequence that after arrival the brand new 747s sat on the ground at Heathrow for almost a year until agreement was reached. As a result of this delay the British flag carrier had not fared well in comparison with other transatlantic operators. Most of those employing the 747 recorded a marked traffic growth, much of which was due to the considerable increase in capacity available. Passenger reaction to the wide-bodied type was mixed, but on the whole they were impressed. Any lack of enthusiasm was usually caused by the poor level of reliability suffered in the early period, but as the improved engines were introduced such criticism was forgotten. As the first operator, Pan Am found several service snags during the first six months. An insufficient number of cabin staff were carried initially and the food trollies were unsatisfactory. It also became apparent that passengers tended to walk around far more than anticipated, thereby hindering the smooth distribution of sustenance. These strollers could also cause embarrassment to others attempting to reach the distant facilities with all speed!

Needless to say, ground handling created plenty of its own problems. New methods were devised at airports so that the greatly increased volume of travellers could be processed

(continued overleaf)

(continued)
be, because in mid-December the young carrier went into liquidation after operations spanning less than six months. For G-HIHO it meant the start of another spate of inactivity, this time in Brussels with Sabena, the company entrusted with the 747's maintenance. Attempts to relaunch Highland Express failed, thereby sealing the fate of yet another airline. In due course the 747 left Europe for service with Air Pacific.
Alan J. Wright

Far right
Formed in 1987, Luxembourg-based Lionair's two 747s became a familiar sight in the UK from the beginning of the 1988 summer season after the company began flying transatlantic ITs. Also involved in the contract was the American operator, Orion Air, which explains the presence of this carrier's name on the forward fuselage of LX-GCV. No stranger to Britain, this machine was one of the early batch to see service with Pan Am in 1970 registered N770PA, the identity it retained until transferring to Lionair.
Alan J. Wright

efficiently. It only took a couple of 747 loads to arrive together in order to create chaos. Baggage arrangements had to be reorganised; likewise, caterers had to think in terms of far greater numbers than hitherto. All this happened at a time when there was a general recession looming in the travel industry which quickly removed any prospect of one of the promised benefits expected at the dawn of the wide-bodied era. Instead of the confidently forecast reductions, fares were in fact increased, due in the main to the fuel crisis of 1973. Therefore it was some years before the airlines adjusted themselves to the effects of the 747's arrival, but long before the end of the decade the mighty machine was fully established and accepted by operators and public alike.

A new breed of long-distance traveller was created in the 1970s. European sun-seekers now progressed from the short range IT flights to transatlantic sorties on board the 747s heading for Florida or California. Cheaper fares began to have their effect at last and the capacious cabins were frequently filled. With the introduction of in-flight movies to provide some entertainment during the journey so came the demand for window blinds to be lowered. No longer was it possible to view the snow covered Rockies as the 747 sped along at 35,000 ft without becoming unpopular with the captive audience in the mobile cinema. Maybe it would be better to employ some windowless freighters for those who feel compelled to watch the silver screen.

Boeing had introduced a cargo version early in the type's career, which had first flown on 30 November 1970. Lufthansa became the first carrier to take delivery the following March. An upward-opening nose door provided ease of loading and the design also incorporated a special system for stowing the freight on to the deck. World Airways took delivery of the first convertible 747 in April 1973, only a month or so after its maiden flight. This variant could be used in an all-passenger, all-cargo or combination mode to suit the carrier's needs. As an extension of this theme the mixed load option was assisted by the addition of a large cargo door in the port side of the rear fuselage. This arrangement subsequently became a retrospective modification for airliners previously restricted to carrying passengers. To meet the special requirements of Japan Air Lines, Boeing developed a short range model known as the 747SR. Both structural changes and strengthening were necessary to provide the robustness

for the abnormally high number of landing cycles demanded by the carrier's operations. At the same time, high-density seating was installed to allow 516 travellers to be accommodated.

More obvious changes were visible on the 747SP. Announced in 1973, this model was intended for use on lower-density routes or long range sectors requiring non-stop flights. A reduction in fuselage length of 46 ft 7 in (14.2 m) and an increase in size of the tail surfaces produced a tubby appearance when it entered service with Pan Am in the spring of 1976. Subsequently, several notable record-breaking long distance trips were completed by the airline's machines. Sales were not particularly spectacular and production ceased in July 1982 after 46 aircraft had been built. However, the manufacturer has considered applying the latest technology to the variant in order to create a possible competitor for the Airbus A340 and MD-11.

A more eager reception awaited the series 300 in the mid-1980s. In this case Boeing stretched the familiar upper deck of the standard 747 so that 69 seats could be carried in this compartment. Although produced as a new aircraft, the modified section could also be provided on customers' own machines if required. Internally the method of access to the upper cabin was changed from a spiral to an orthodox straight stairway. Even as this version entered service in 1983 the manufacturer was already developing an updated 747 with an emphasis on efficiency and range rather than increased capacity. When launched as the series 400 it almost immediately out-sold the 300, many operators preferring to bypass the latter to await the latest offering. While retaining the stretched upper deck, the newcomer acquired an increase in wingspan of 12 ft plus the more obvious addition of a 6 ft-tall winglet at each tip. These changes are designed to produce a fuel reduction per passenger mile of 7% compared with the 300's performance. A considerable degree of modernisation has been introduced on to the flight deck which is now designed to be occupied by a crew of two. With typical Boeing showmanship, the 400 was rolled out at Everett on 26 January 1988 while bathed in a wall of laser lights before an estimated 10,000 guests. Slightly later than expected, its first flight took place on 29 April to enable the test programme to begin. After certification the Pratt & Whitney PW4000 powered aircraft was destined for Northwest

Right

It is customary for both cargo and passengers to travel inside the cabin of any airliner, the 747 normally being no exception to this rule. Indeed when N9668 entered service with American Airlines in 1970 it followed these traditions without deviation. Suddenly in 1974 this all changed. At the time the National Aeronautics and Space Administration (NASA) required the services of a transport for its Orbiters without dismantling the substantial airframes for the journey. Chosen for this new role, N9668 was despatched to Boeing for a variety of modifications, the most obvious being the addition of three pylons on the cabin roof and a fin at the tips of the tailplane. Reregistered N905NA, the 747 began its new career in 1977 with a series of test flights from Edwards AFB with the un-manned Orbiter *Enterprise* firmly attached. Then followed three sorties with the astronaut crew on board to give them the opportunity to try out the flight system without actual separation. Finally, on 12 August the Orbiter was released from the mother ship to make its own somewhat faster descent from 24,000 ft for an unpowered landing back at

(continued on next page)

Airlines towards the end of the year. Ten aircraft were ordered by this carrier in October 1985 when it became the launch customer, an example later followed by a further 17 airlines to bring the total number of orders to 118 by the roll-out date. Lufthansa expects to receive the second 400 off the line in March 1989 followed by Cathay Pacific a month later. Power for the latter pair will be provided by General Electric CF6-80C2s and Rolls-Royce RB211-524Gs respectively. Only two months after its maiden trip aloft, the variant was able to claim the world record for the heaviest aircraft take-off. On 27 June it lifted 892,450 lb from Moses Lake Airport, Washington, some 44,100 lb above the normal weight.

So the well-proven giant looks set to take the industry into the next century. No doubt further models will become available as the need arises, with a full length upper deck extension capable of carrying up to 700 passengers a distinct possibility, but at present there is no demand for such capacity. By mid-1988 the total number of orders for the 747 had reached 868 from 72 airlines. Operators of the type at some time or other include:

Aer Lingus, Aerolineas Argentinas, Air Afrique, Air Algerie, Air Canada, Air France, Air Gabon, Air India, Air Jamaica, Air Lanka, Air Madagascar, Air Mauritius, Air National, Air New Zealand, Air Pacific, Air Portugal, Air Siam, Air Zaire, Alia/Royal Jordanian, Alitalia, All Nippon, American Airlines, Avianca, BOAC/British Airways, British Airtours, British Caledonian, CAAC, Cameroon Airlines, Cargolux, Cathay Pacific, China Airlines, Condor, Continental Airlines, CP Air/Canadian Airlines International, Delta Air Lines, Dominicana, Eastern Air Lines, Egyptair, El Al, Evergreen International, Flying Tiger, Garuda Indonesian, Gulf Air, Hawaii Express, Highland Express, Iberia, Icelandair, Iraqi Airways, Iran Air, Iranian Air Force, Japan Air Lines, Japan Asia, Jet 24, KLM, Kenya Airways, Korean Airlines, Kuwait Airways, Lionair, Lufthansa, Malaysian Airline System, Martinair, Metro International, Middle East Airlines, NASA, National Airlines, Nigeria Airways, Northwest Orient, Olympic Airways, Overseas National, Pakistan International, Pan Am, People Express, Philippine Airlines, Qantas, Royal Air Maroc, Sabena, SAS, Saudia, Saudi Royal Flight, Scanair, Seaboard World, Singapore Airlines, South African Airways, Swan Airlines, Swissair, Thai International, Tower Air, Trans International/Transamerica, Trans Mediterranean Airways, Trans World Airlines, United Airlines, United Parcels, USAF, UTA, Varig, Viasa, Virgin Atlantic, Wardair and World Airways. Representatives of some of these are to be found within this book.

base. With tests complete, NASA's unique 747 was thereafter used to ferry the operational Shuttles to the Kennedy launch site in readiness for their exploits, thereby playing an important part in the American space programme.
Peter R. March

Below left
At 10.00 hrs on 7 June 1983, the 747-123 N905NA began its take-off roll along Stansted's Runway 23 to carry the Orbiter *Enterprise* back to the US. As it climbed away there were feelings of relief on the ground that the three-day visit had been so successful. The event certainly caught the imagination of the public who turned out in their hundreds of thousands to choke roads for miles around the Essex airport where a truly carnival atmosphere was created. Many of the anti-airport campaigners used the opportunity to raise funds for repairs to a church roof or two by the sale of home-made rock buns, many of which could have served as material for the renovation. But it was the 747 and its passenger which were deservedly the real attraction to provide a sight few will ever forget.
Alan J. Wright

Right

With 1986 its 60th year of operations, Northwest Orient sponsored the Fighter Meet held at North Weald over the last weekend in June. As the name implies, aircraft of a more warlike nature predominate at this type of function, but an exception was made on this occasion. On both days the airline sent its newly delivered 747-251B N637US to execute some flypasts with a difference. Ambling along at a modest speed, it contrived to formate with Air Atlantique's DC-3 G-AMPY which was suitably adorned in Northwest livery and struggling to match its mighty descendant's progress. During other passes, the 747 was joined by a variety of piston engined fighters, including several Spitfires, a P-47, a Kittyhawk and a Corsair with others valiantly trying to keep up with their unusual formation leader. Dwarfed by the sheer bulk of the airliner, the fighters buzzed around, their pilots thoroughly enjoying this rare opportunity for such an escapade. There is little doubt that the billed appearance of a 747 at a display attracts the crowds in a similar manner to Concorde, the Red Arrows and the Battle of Britain Memorial Flight.

Peter R. March

Left
Northwest's normal activity involves the operation of a vast network of routes throughout the US and Canada, which was considerably increased with the takeover of Republic Airlines in 1986. One of the country's oldest carriers, it was founded in 1926 as Northwest Airlines, but in view of its interests in the East, Orient was added to the title in 1934. Apart from its domestic work, Northwest – as it again became in 1986 – still flies on routes crossing the Pacific, but also includes transatlantic sectors nowadays to link the US with Copenhagen, Dublin, Frankfurt, London, Oslo, Prestwick and Stockholm. Forty passenger and freighter 747s are on strength and the airline became the launch customer for the series 400 in 1985, the first of which should be delivered at the end of 1988. Still with its Northwest Orient titles, N623US is seen landing at Miami, an airport frequently visited by the airline.
Colin Wright

Right

After over eight years with Alitalia as I-DEMB, this 747-243B was returned to Boeing in 1980 for a series of leases lasting until the end of 1984 when the machine was finally purchased by People Express to become N605PE. This carrier was formed in April 1980, its aim being to offer low-cost, high-frequency domestic services in the eastern part of the US; growth came rapidly to take it into transatlantic operations on 26 May 1983. From a single 747 at the outset, the number of the type in service with the carrier steadily grew until eight were on strength in 1986. During the course of the year People Express found itself with increasing financial problems resulting in its sale to the Texas Air Corporation. Consequently, by early 1987 all its activities and fleet had been merged with those of Continental Airlines. Under the new ownership both logo and titles were quickly replaced, but the repainting of the airframe was not attempted at that stage. Accordingly the Continental 747s flew with their People Express livery and registrations throughout the year, but during 1988 they were due to acquire new identities, N33021 being allocated to the depicted specimen.

Robbie Shaw

Right

Edinburgh is seldom visited by 747s, but on this occasion an Alitalia machine (I-DEMG) arrived. Most of the larger UK airports can handle wide-bodied aircraft providing small numbers are involved, but it is not economic to hold numerous sets of the specialist equipment required for each type likely to appear. When weather conditions force diversions, it is therefore necessary to spread the load as evenly as possible between the airports with the means to cope.

British Airports Authority

Bottom left

Northwest has a long history, but the Colombian national airline, Avianca, stretches back even further to the founding of SCADTA in 1919. Based at Bogata, the carrier now undertakes a wide range of domestic services plus links with North and Central America. Long-haul European flights are offered to Frankfurt, Madrid and Paris for which purpose a 747 is employed. This is now registered HK-2980X, but from its delivery in 1979 until 1983 it carried the identity HK-2300 as in the photograph.

Colin Wright

Right
It is a long time since Pan Am's 747-121 N735PA first crossed the Atlantic during a proving flight on 12 January 1970, three days after its delivery to the airline. Since then the machine has been a regular commuter between the US and Europe, although during that time its livery has changed several times – the latest variation ensuring that short-sighted passengers can find it.
Alan J. Wright

Far right
An ex-Braniff machine, the 1970-built 747-127 N601BN is operated by Tower Air both on schedules and charters. Formed in August 1982, the airline took over the routes previously flown by Metro International from New York to Brussels, Oslo, Stockholm and Tel Aviv.
Robbie Shaw

Right

If 747s are not loaded direct from the terminal building then the alternative is usually to employ buses to ferry the travellers to the aircraft. With conditions somewhat akin to the London Underground in a rush hour, this first part of the journey is often undertaken in a standing position until each vehicle in turn arrives at the wide-bodied stairway. If only one door is in use on the aircraft, boarding can take some time, although in wet and windy weather the process speeds up considerably. This picture of a TWA machine shows off the shape of the 747 particularly well.

British Airports Authority

Left

As one of America's leading supplemental carriers, for many years World Airways offered a world-wide range of charters using a variety of aircraft types. In 1973 three 747 combis began work with the company, one of which was N747WA. Although painted in the airline's livery when delivered, the machine spent more time on lease to other carriers than it did with its own operator. In fact for almost five years it stayed with Pan Am as N535PA before returning to World Airways in December 1979. Strangely it never reverted to its full original identity, adopting the suffix WR instead. From this point it was not reregistered although its temporary detachments continued to take it into the hands of National Airlines, Evergreen International, Flying Tigers and Air India. For most of its career it has been used as a freighter, but in a passenger configuration it was equipped with 471 seats. When World Airways drastically reduced its activities in 1986, it restricted its fleet to a few DC-10-30s, so the 747 was never repainted in the new colour scheme chosen by the company.

Boeing

Right
Until the Boeing 747-21AC PH-MCE joined Martinair in the spring of 1987, the airline's long-haul charters were covered by four DC-10-30s. As in the latter case, the newcomer is a combi and when configured for passenger work is equipped with 530 seats. With such a capacity it is also useful for the short European IT sectors in peak periods.
Robbie Shaw

Far right
Air India's VT-EGC is almost at the end of its long journey from Bombay as it crosses the perimeter fence at Heathrow. Last of the airline's 747s to be delivered by Boeing, it arrived some nine years after the first had joined the fleet in 1971. European appearances are not confined to the UK since several other centres on the continent are included in the company's network of routes. India's flag carrier has scheduled links with North America where the gateways are at New York, Montreal and Toronto, while both Perth and Sydney in Australia receive regular visits by the 747s.
Peter R. March

Right

At Amsterdam's Schiphol airport security is often achieved at the perimeter by a series of wide ditches. Fences are therefore unnecessary at these locations which enables uncluttered pictures to be obtained from various vantage points. Since the land alongside the runways is leased to local farmers, aircraft appear to taxy through the middle of a series of small-holdings, the crops varying from cereals to potatoes. Needless to say no livestock is permitted, although the stretches of water provide a home for a multitude of noisy toads. There are several periods in the day when the KLM 747s are particularly active and it therefore does not take long for the fleet to parade before the patient onlooker. In this case the subject is PH-BUC which has been with the airline since May 1971 and is not one of those earmarked to receive the stretched upper deck modification. On the contrary, it will be one of the machines released when the series 406s are delivered in 1989.

Alan J. Wright

Left
Naturally the most common livery to be found on 747s at London is that of British Airways. Some 35 examples made up the fleet in early 1988, but to these will be added the machines inherited by the take-over of British Caledonian. Further additions will occur in the spring of 1989 when the first of the new series 400s arrives, but at this time a start will be made on the retirement of the early fleet members, so the actual numbers on strength will not increase appreciably.
Peter R. March

Right
In November 1970 Sabena took delivery of OO-SGA, the first of a pair of 747-129s. After three years or so both were given a combi layout with a side cargo door for use on the airline's North American and West African services. In October 1986 Sabena began a Brussels-Gatwick- Atlanta service in association with British Caledonian. Originally the agreement was for a one year period, but in fact the services were continued under a temporary permit until the end of March 1988. With the change of partner it is doubtful if the arrangement would have continued anyway.
George W. Pennick

Far right
Jordanian airline Alia was the source of British Caledonian's second Boeing 747 which arrived at Gatwick on 18 March 1985. Still registered JY-AFB, it departed to Paris Orly a few days later for a repaint and a change of identity to G-HUGE. After a lengthy refurbishment the combi eventually entered service on the company's revived Gatwick-New York route on 25 June – a daily commitment which kept the machine fully occupied. After more than two years work for BCal on this and other sectors, it became a victim of the British Airways take-over in late 1987.
Robbie Shaw

Right
**Delivered in 1985, D-ABYZ
has since been operated by
Lufthansa on its long-haul
sectors. Like most of its two
dozen colleagues in the
fleet it is fitted with a side
cargo door for mixed
working.**
Lufthansa

Far right
**Becoming a 747 operator in
1973, for the next 10 years
or so Olympic Airways
found two aircraft
sufficient for use on its
transatlantic and Far East
services. In 1985 the oldest
of the pair was sold to TWA,
but by this time
negotiations had been
completed with Singapore
Airlines for the purchase of
three younger aircraft.
Appropriately, the carrier's
livery prominently displays
the 'six rings' symbol of the
Olympic games, but
otherwise the colour
scheme used is not
particularly imaginative.**
Boeing

Right

For many years the brightly coloured airliners of CP Air were a familiar sight at the major UK airports from where a large number of Canadian ITs were flown using both DC-10s and Boeing 747s. Of the latter, C-FCRE was one of four acquired in 1973–74 to serve the carrier for over 10 years. A policy of standardisation in 1985 found the quartet leaving the Canadian company for a new career with Pakistan International, 'Romeo Echo' becoming the first to leave in December of that year. Exchanged with an equal number of DC-10s, the newcomers confusingly adopted the same identities as the departing Boeings.

Alan J. Wright

Far right

After a modest entry into the international scheduled scene in March 1945, TAP's network steadily grew until it included transatlantic routes. TAP joined the wide-bodied club in 1972 when it took delivery of CS-TJA, the first of two 747s ordered. Eventually the fleet comprised four of the type, but the second pair did not remain for long before joining Pakistan International. In 1980 the airline was renamed Air Portugal.

Boeing

Wherever El Al's airliners operate there is a considerable security effort mounted. At some airports a procession is formed, with armoured vehicles, positioned fore and aft of the taxying 747 during its journey from and to the active runway, remaining in attendance during its stay at the terminal. Fortunately such precautions are not considered necessary by any other carrier including those of Arab origin. Ironically the Israeli aircraft often park alongside those belonging to supposedly hostile nations and indeed it is not uncommon for cargo to be moved from one machine to another for onward transportation.
British Airports Authority

Top left

Alia's 747 fleet did not grow a great deal after the first two were delivered in April and May 1977. In fact it was 1981 before another was acquired with all three employed thereafter on the longer transatlantic sectors and some of those within Europe. However, TriStars began to replace the larger type in 1981 resulting in the departure of two 747s to British Caledonian in 1985 and 1987. This left the single specimen (JY-AFA) to ply the New York route for much of its time. In the mid-1980s the airline embarked on a painting spree in an effort to portray a new image. Eventually, after many trial schemes, the chosen livery was predominantly brown and the Royal Jordanian identity was emphasised rather than just that of Alia. In the illustration 'Foxtrot Alpha' is wearing its original 1977 colours.
Boeing

Bottom left

Since taking delivery of the 747 combi CN-RME in 1978, Royal Air Maroc has used it mainly for its transatlantic schedules. These do not over-burden the machine unduly so it also makes regular sorties to the Middle East, an area which creates several high-density routes as a result of ITs designed for pilgrims.
Boeing

Right

Since South African Airways began 747 operations in the early 1970s, the airline has introduced some impressive schedules including non-stop sectors between Johannesberg and European cities. Its 747s roam far and wide but are also to be found on shorter high-density routes. Since ZS-SAN was delivered in October 1971 its livery has been subtly changed although the basic colours remain the same. Nowadays the aircraft carries the letters SAA along the left forward fuselage while on the opposite side the Afrikaanse equivalent SAL appears. On the fin the springbok representation now leaves no room for any other decoration, but the whole design gives the fleet a more modern appearance.
Boeing

Left
To earn its keep a 747 has to spend the majority of its life in the air. Pushbacks across a well-lit airport apron before the start of another night flight were therefore common occurrences for Lufthansa's D-ABYC, one of the airline's first batch of three aircraft delivered in 1970. Its life with the German carrier lasted until January 1979 when it joined Aer Lingus as EI-BED to be configured to carry 468 passengers in an all-tourist layout. During its stay with the Irish airline it has also spent short spells with Air Algerie and Air Jamaica.
Lufthansa

Far left
As a result of the Falklands
disagreement, Aerolineas
Argentinas no longer serves
London. Nevertheless its
747s are still to be seen
elsewhere in Europe with
flights crossing the south
Atlantic to include Paris,
Frankfurt, Madrid, Rome
and Zurich in the coverage.
For anyone with an
irresistible urge to visit this
South American country it
is therefore necessary to
travel first to one of these
cities. Six 747-200s are on
the strength of the national
carrier, although the after
effects of the 1982 war
necessitated several leases
due to diminishing traffic.

Left
Considering the overall
proportions of the 747, the
flightdeck is quite compact.
Looking ahead, the pilots'
view is akin to that from an
attic window while trying to
get the ground floor on to
the runway without it
becoming the basement!
This particular example is
still equipped with electro-
mechanical instruments
but the new 747s have
moved into the age of
cathode ray tube displays
and the associated
electronic control aids. At
the same time the new
cockpit is designed for
operation by two pilots
alone unlike the current
models which all have the
services of a flight engineer.

Only three 747-200s are employed by the Chinese national carrier, CAAC, B-2450 being delivered in the spring of 1987. To the right of its fin can be seen the tail of N1304E (now B-2452), one of four SP variants also flown by the airline. With this somewhat plain livery the most outstanding feature is the large national flag carried on the fin. Scribed in Chinese along the fuselage sides is the airline's title, but, for the benefit of those unable to read the language, CAAC is repeated in small characters in the vicinity of the flight deck. Those adept with a paint brush will have plenty of practice when the airline takes up the identity of Air China.
Robbie Shaw

Left
Formed in 1946, Cathay Pacific employed DC-3s in those early days, launching scheduled services two years later. Now recognised as the Hong Kong flag carrier despite being privately owned, the company serves centres in the Middle and Far East, Australia, Europe and North America. Only wide-bodied aircraft are now used, the first of the 747s joining the fleet in 1980. Eight passenger carrying series 200s are now on strength, of which VR-HIE was the fifth to arrive. Another pair perform their duties as freighters while the latest additions have been the stretched upper deck variant, the type which maintains the longer range sectors. Although the runway has water alongside it, the mountain in the background confirms that the 747 is not landing at London City!
Robbie Shaw

Right
Clustered around Tokyo's Narita terminal are four of the 60 or so 747s of all models operated by Japan Air Lines. In the foreground is JA8115, one of five standard series 100s in service while at the rear of the group a stretched upper deck series 300 can be seen. Red and black are the only colours used in the company's livery which, on the upper surfaces of the wings, includes the familiar red disc generally associated with the country. JAL operates over a large network of international routes, but lost its monopoly in 1986 when All Nippon introduced services to Guam. However, as compensation the Japanese national carrier was able to launch its first new domestic sectors since 1972. From April 1986, non-stop flights have been offered between Tokyo and both London and Paris.
Robbie Shaw

After some years Philippine Airlines has adopted a more modern livery for its fleet which includes four Boeing 747s – all of which entered service in 1980. Based on the national flag, the fin marking differs from that previously carried by the addition of a sun-burst design appearing from behind the red segment. It was intended to signify a new beginning for the country at the end of a 14-year-long dictatorship. In a similar manner to its three colleagues, N742PR has continued to be identified by a US registration rather than by one allocated in the Philippine's series. Their duties take them on long-haul international sectors to the Middle East and Europe where regular visits are made to Amsterdam, Athens, Frankfurt, London/ Gatwick, Paris, Rome and Zurich. Schedules are also flown to the west coast of the US at Los Angeles and the Pacific island of Hawaii.
Robbie Shaw

Top right

Externally there is little to distinguish JA8152 from any other standard 747 in the 100 series. However, the 747SR was developed as a short range, high-density version aimed particularly at the Japanese market. All Nippon operates domestic and regional services with the type which it first took on strength at the end of 1978. Since then a total of 17 have joined the fleet which has steadily shed the pale blue livery worn for some years by such as JA8152.
Robbie Shaw

Bottom right

All Nippon's latest colour scheme is well illustrated by JA8133, which was in fact the first 747SR-81 to join the airline in December 1978. Formed in 1958 from the merger of Far Eastern Airlines and Japan Helicopter & Aeroplane Transport Co, All Nippon has since become the country's largest airline, although it was March 1986 before its first international scheduled service was launched to link Tokyo with Guam. Routes to both Los Angeles and Washington followed in July and in due course the carrier hopes to serve European cities. Already six 747-200s are on strength for this type of operation and on order are 11 of the new series 400.
Robbie Shaw

As could be expected, Nippon Cargo Airlines (NCA) is associated with All Nippon, but in this case its fleet contains three 747 freighters with a fourth machine on order. Delivered in February 1985, JA8168 was the second aircraft to arrive before scheduled cargo services were started on 8 May. The company was actually formed in September 1978, the lengthy delay in beginning operations being due to a civil aviation policy review conducted by the Japanese authorities. New York and San Francisco are now visited by NCA's aircraft six times each week, while Hong Kong is the destination on two occasions in the same period, all services radiating from Tokyo.
Robbie Shaw

Right

In addition to a wide range of domestic and international passenger schedules, Korean Air also uses its four 747 freighters for regular flights to airports in Europe, the US and the Far East. Seen touching down at Hong Kong is HL7452, which has also spent some time on lease to Saudia since its delivery in 1980.
Robbie Shaw

Far right

The company which formed as Seaboard and Western in 1947 later adopted the title Seaboard World before going on to become one of America's leading cargo carriers by providing regular international services. It soon found itself operating on behalf of other airlines such as Viasa and Saudia, carrying the additional titles on the fuselage alongside those of its owner. However, from 1977 Flying Tiger Line steadily acquired an interest in the company until finally, on 1 October 1980, Seaboard World was completely taken over and merged into its rival. Quick to disappear was the smart gold and white livery, while new identities were allocated to the fleet, N701SW becoming N811FT with its new owner.

Right

Simple but effective is the livery of Flying Tigers, the first all-cargo airline in the US. Formed in 1945, the present title was adopted a year later. For many years the carrier confined most of its work to the American continent and trans-Pacific scheduled freight services. In order to expand its interests across the Atlantic to Europe, the company acquired Seaboard World in October 1980, thereby gaining access to this new market for its large fleet which was further increased in size by the newcomers. One of the 747s affected was N704SW which nowadays flies in FTL's livery with the identity N814FT.
Robbie Shaw

Now France's largest independent airline, UTA was created in 1963 by the amalgamation of UAT and TAI, a pair of carriers dedicated to maintaining links with the former French Territories in West Africa. These destinations still account for much of UTA's work with 25 different points visited both on passenger and cargo services. However, its activities are not confined to this area since its network also embraces the Far East, Australia, New Zealand, some of the Pacific islands and the west coast of the US. A large volume of freight is handled by the company which employs the 747 F-GBOX exclusively for this work backed up by four combi machines – two each of the 200 and 300 series.
Robbie Shaw

When granted independence, the former French colonies in
Africa found it impossible to own an airline individually for
financial reasons. Nevertheless, to ensure survival it was
essential that air transport was readily available, so as a
solution 11 states pooled resources in March 1961 to create
Air Afrique as their official carrier. Services have since been
maintained on regional routes throughout Africa as well as
providing regular links with France where strong ties still
exist. Air Afrique began its association with the 747 in October
1980 when it received the freighter TU-TAP for use on its
cargo services. Gainful employment was found until March
1984 when a series of leases saw the end of the machine's
service with the airline. However, it is anticipated that a combi
version will be joining the fleet to renew the carrier's
acquaintance with the type.
Boeing

Left
This specialised freighter version of the 747 was developed early in the type's career, flying for the first time on 20 November 1971. Certificated during the following March, it was almost immediately delivered to Lufthansa the German national carrier becoming the first to operate the variant. An increasing number of airlines are taking up the option to have a side cargo door installed to speed up further the loading and unloading process. A regular visitor at major airports around the world, special lifting devices are used to raise the freight pallets to the 747's floor level at which point the aircraft's own system can be employed to handle and stow the load.

Far left
Few personnel are necessary during the loading of a 747 freighter providing the lifting devices are available. Air France, which is one of the larger carriers undertaking freight work in addition to its extensive passenger operations, employs seven specialist aircraft, each of which also has the side door fitted. Stansted has a growing involvement in cargo handling and it is at the Essex airport that F-BPVR was seen ingesting its latest consignments.
British Airports Authority

Left
Rolls-Royces are loaded onboard Japan Air Lines 747-246F (SCD) JA8171.
BAA/Arthur Kemsley

Right

Stansted by night: Flying Tiger Line 747-249F(SCD) N810FT *Clifford G. Groh* prepares to receive a consignment of cargo. At present the apron provided for such activities can only accommodate one 747 so a speedy turn-round is essential.
BAA/Arthur Kemsley

Far right

Showing off its distinctive squat appearance is the first of Braniff's 747SPs. One of the older and larger US airlines, Braniff ordered three with deliveries to begin in 1979 – October of that year marking the arrival of N603BN. Orange was a popular colour with the company although it was by no means standard for all the fleet. Used for a short time on the carrier's long range non-stop sectors, the SPs were not destined to remain long in Braniff's employ. After barely a year N603BN retired for a period of storage with Boeing which finally ended in 1985 when it took up a new life in Oman. In the meantime its former owner had gone into liquidation and the fleet had dispersed anyway.
Boeing

Far left
During the early 1980s Air Mauritius employed Boeing 707s on its international sectors, but the need to offer more modern equipment found the carrier leasing a 747SP from South African Airways with another from the same source joining the airline in 1987 to become 3B-NAJ. The type is used on European routes which includes those serving London, Paris, Rome and Zurich.
George W. Pennick

Left
In some States wars tend to interrupt normal activities, but Iran's national carrier has managed to operate its 747SP-86s without a great deal of attention from the opposition. Iran Air became the second airline to take delivery of the variant in March 1976, that illustrated (EP-IAB) following two months later. Surprisingly there are travellers in sufficient numbers to justify three visits per week to the UK.
British Airports Authority

Far left
One of the current users of the 747SP, Syrianair was an early customer for the variant, taking delivery of YK-AHA in May 1976. This was followed two months later by the second and last. Subsequently, the pair have been used on the airline's longer routes, although these are relatively few and do not extend across the Atlantic. Although the national flag is reproduced on the side of the rear cabin, the carrier's livery does not include any red or black, but instead uses blue for the cheat line and fin.
British Airports Authority

Left
For many years the Australian flag carrier has operated an all-Boeing fleet made up of 747 variants and the 767. Included in the former are a pair of 747SPs which were acquired by the airline in 1981 for use on the long trans-Pacific services to the west coast of America. First to arrive was VH-EAA wearing the livery of the period, but since delivery the airline has adopted a more modern all-white scheme with a red fin and rear fuselage.
Boeing

Unlike its neighbour, CAAC, China Airlines is less reluctant to display its title in English using letters as large as those employed for the national language. As the national carrier for the Republic of China based in Taiwan, a number of 747s are operated on international scheduled services which include routes to New York, Los Angeles and Amsterdam, the latter being the only European city currently visited. Amongst the fleet are four of the SP version, N4508H being one of them. Originally this was destined to become B-1882, but because the machine was leased it adopted a US identity instead, a practice which is not uncommon nowadays.
Robbie Shaw

Left
The 747 approaching in this view is N141UA, an SP belonging to United Airlines. Back in 1975 it was the second of the type to fly and was part of the batch ordered by Pan Am. For some months it remained with the manufacturer, but with tests complete it joined its intended owner in May 1976 as N531PA. Thirteen SPs eventually joined the airline and were used on a number of long haul routes until circumstances forced Pan Am to sell some of its assets. These included all the Pacific operations and some 18 aircraft, the majority of which were the 747SPs. Therefore, in February 1986 United formally took over the machines, in due course reregistering them in its own sequence.
Robbie Shaw

Left
Swissair was a launch customer for the stretched upper deck variant of the 747, taking delivery of its first (HB-IGD) in March 1983. Equipped with a side cargo door, this combi version is configured with 261 seats in three classes while its freight load varies with the routes upon which it is employed. Together with the three others operated by the national carrier, HB-IGD is normally employed on the long range services between Zurich and North America or the Far East. When delivered the series 300s displaced two 747s which had been with the airline since early 1971.
Robbie Shaw

Above
Appropriately, the stretched upper deck 747-300s belonging to Singapore Airlines have all had the inscription 'Big Top' painted to the rear of the flight deck. In most cases the aircraft carry a US registration which incorporates the last two letters of the mark allocated by the Singapore authorities but which remained unused. For example the specimen depicted is identified as N123KJ rather than 9V-SKJ as originally intended. It is one of 14 in service with SIA which maintains a policy of operating a young fleet. Routes to some 50 destinations are now served by the carrier which did not begin operations until October 1972.
Robbie Shaw

Japan Air Lines also favours the use of the 747SR high-density version for its domestic services, but unlike All Nippon the airline has some series 300s in its fleet. Used for the long international sectors, JAL was an early customer for the variant, taking delivery of N212JL in 1983. Later the extended cabin also proved an attractive idea for increasing still further the capacity of the 747SR. Two were therefore ordered for delivery in 1988, each aircraft having the ability to carry 563 passengers. Upon arrival the newcomers were expected to release some of the older specimens for relatively early retirement – an event brought about by the high number of landings made by machines used on short sector working.
Peter R. March

Amongst the assorted types operated by Saudia are 10 747-300s, HZ-AIT being the last of the batch when delivered in 1986. As the largest Middle East carrier, the airline operates scheduled passenger and cargo services to points in the Far East, Africa, Europe and the US. The daily sorties between Jeddah and London are all covered by the large capacity 747s, such is the traffic generated. Whatever the practical benefits derived from the extended upper cabin, the classic lines of the original 747 design are difficult to improve.
Robbie Shaw

Right

Two for the price of one – a shot achieved by zooming the lens rather than moving the 747. After 1992 it may serve to bring back fond memories of the days when duty-frees made such views possible even without a camera!

Far right

British Airways is unlikely to change its livery before the first of the new 747-436s arrives in 1989. However, this artist's impression also serves to illustrate the two main external differences between the newcomer and the earlier variants. Following the popular fashion, the aircraft has grown a winglet at each tip and also incorporates the extended upper deck introduced on the preceeding series 300. Registrations in the range commencing G-BNLA have been reserved for the newcomers.
Boeing

The end.
Lufthansa

BOEING 757/767

ROBBIE SHAW

First published 1992

INTRODUCTION

Although the Boeing 737 is now the world's best selling jet airliner two other Boeing twin-jets, the 757 and 767, are also selling very well. An increasing number of airlines now operate both the 757 and 767, aircraft which provide the flexibility to service hub-and-spoke operations as well as long range routes. Another added factor being that these aircraft have a common flightdeck, which permits the two-man crew to have a common type rating and fly all variants of both models.

The sleek-looking 757 is at home in both the high density short-haul arena and the intercontinental long-haul routes. It is also proving popular with charter operators. This quiet fuel efficient aircraft can seat 180-230 passengers, depending on configuration, and has a range of almost 4,000 nautical miles. It is also finding an increasing role in short to medium-range freight operations.

The 767 meanwhile is available in both the 767-200 and 767-300 models, both variants have extended range versions for use on intercontinental routes. The 767-200 seats 181 passengers and has a range of 6,700nm, whilst the 767-300 series, which is 21ft longer, offers a 20% increase in passenger capacity and 44% in freight capacity. The 767-300 extended range variant can carry 218 passengers 6,200nm.

It was in 1978 that Boeing announced its proposals to build the 757 and 767. The 757 was designed as a replacement for the Boeing 727 in the short/medium-range role, whilst the 767 was destined for transcontinental and intercontinental routes.

The 757 was to be a considerable technological leap from the popular 727. The aircraft has a long thin 727-type fuselage with a prominent tall fin, although the advanced design wing has less sweepback than the 727. The powerplants chosen were the Rolls-Royce RB211-535 and the Pratt & Whitney PW2037 high bypass turbofans, to be mounted in two underwing pods. Internally the aircraft's seating is six abreast with a single aisle. The first order for the 757 was from one of Boeing's best customers, British Airways, who ordered 19 aircraft with options on a further 18. This was quickly followed by Eastern who ordered 21 with options on 24. This was sufficient for Boeing and the following year, 1979, production of the aircraft started.

The prototype 757 was rolled out at Boeing's Renton factory on 13 January 1982, and its maiden flight took place soon afterwards on 19 February. This aircraft was powered by two Rolls-Royce RB211-535Cs, the first time Boeing had launched a jet airliner with a non-American engine — the 757 had set a record already! This, and the next four aircraft off the production line, were used in the test and certification programme. Only 10 months after the maiden flight of the type, Eastern took delivery of its first aircraft. Less than two weeks later, on 1 January 1983, that aircraft entered service — an amazing feat. British Airways received its first aircraft soon afterwards, entering service on 9 February. The basic version of the aircraft is the 757-200 series, and the next two customers, American and Delta, both ordered this variant, albeit powered by the Pratt & Whitney engine.

The next variant produced was the 757-200ER extended range, with Royal Brunei Airlines being the first customer. It received its first aircraft in May 1986, and the airline's second appeared at the first ever Indonesia Air Show prior to delivery. Royal Brunei now uses its 757s on services to Europe. Early in 1986 two other versions were announced by Boeing, the 757-200PF and 757-200 Combi. The Combi has a cargo door on the port side of the forward fuselage and can be used in a mixed passenger/cargo fit. Royal Nepal Airlines was the launch customer for the Combi variant. The aircraft was received late in 1988, complementing the carrier's 757-200 on services to Hong Kong and Europe. The 757-200PF (Package Freighter) also has a cargo door but, as it does not carry passengers, the windows have been deleted. This variant can carry up to 15 standard cargo 'igloos' on the main deck and was quickly ordered by United Parcel Service with an initial order for 20 aircraft. Ethiopian Airlines, Challenge Air Cargo and Zambia Airways also operate this variant.

Whilst the 757 was being manufactured at Renton, production of the 767 was gathering momentum 30 miles away at Boeing's Everett plant. The 767 is not unlike the A300 Airbus in appearance, with a fuselage length only a few feet longer than the 757, but with a much greater wing span. The seating layout is normally seven abreast with twin aisles. The powerplant chosen by

The sleek lines of the Boeing 757 are evident in this shot of the company demonstrator. *Boeing*

the launch customers was the Pratt & Whitney JT9D turbofan, though General Electric CF6 engines are also being used. The initial variant proposed was the 767-100, however this was dropped and the larger 767-200 became the basic model. The launch customer was United Airlines.

The prototype was rolled out on 4 August 1981 and took to the air for the first time on 26 September, some five months ahead of the 757. The 767 order book filled quickly and the major US carriers, American and Delta, followed United and put the aircraft into service on internal routes. By the end of 1981 Boeing

Left:

The Boeing 767-300 demonstrator seen high over Washington State during a test flight. *Boeing*

had orders for 173 767s, with options on a further 138. The next variant was the extended range 767-200ER with additional fuel tanks in the centre wing section. The first of this variant was delivered to Ethiopian Airlines in June 1984. Two years later a 767-200ER set a new world distance record by a twin-jet commercial aircraft when it flew 6,854nm from Seattle direct to Kuwait for that carrier's national carrier. Five months later, on 1 September, a Lan Chile 767-200ER created another record when it flew the first commercial scheduled service across the Atlantic by a twin-jet. It took only 10hr 12min to fly from Rio de Janeiro to Madrid. In 1983 Boeing announced that a new 'stretched' variant known as the 767-300 was to be produced. This variant could accommodate up to 269 passengers and orders were soon placed by Japan Air Lines, Delta and All Nippon. Inevitably, an extended range variant of the 767-300 was announced in January 1985 and American Airlines was again amongst the first to order this addition to the 767 family. The 767-300ER has also proved popular with a number of other airlines such as Canadian Airlines International, Scandinavian and Gulf Air who use the type on long-haul intercontinental services.

Such is the reliability of modern airliners and engines that the 767 has been instrumental in changing the rules applicable to twin-engined aircraft operating long-haul flights over water (ETOPS - Extended Twin OPerationS). Previously these twin-engined aircraft had to fly routes that would keep them within one hour's flight of an airport should one engine have to be shut down. This rule did not apply to three or four-engined aircraft. In 1985, however, the reliability of aircraft like the 757 and 767 convinced the authorities that this should be extended to two hours. This approval was originally restricted to 767s powered by Pratt & Whitney JT9D-7R4 engines. Trans World Airlines was the first to operate across the Atlantic under these new rules in 1985. This approval was soon extended to 767s powered by General Electric CF6-80A engines and 757s using Rolls-Royce RB211-535E-4 engines. Currently there are six engine and airframe combinations and 17 operators of the Boeing 767 which regularly carry out ETOPS. Indeed most engines on the 767 are now cleared for operations three hours from land and 757 operations are also presently under review with a view to their extension to three hours also.

These Boeing twin-jets have an exceptional safety record, with only one 757 lost to date when it was hit on the ground by another aircraft, whilst the first 767 loss occurred to a Lauda Air aircraft on 26 May 1991 soon after take-off from Bangkok.

As of 21 March 1991 724 Boeing 757s had been ordered by 35 customers, figures for the 767 are 539 aircraft ordered by 46 customers.

The following use, or have ordered, 757s. (Those in brackets no longer operate the type.):

AeroMexico; (Air Aruba); Air Belgium; Air Europa; Air Europa Spa; (Air Europe); Air Holland; Air New Zealand; Air 2000; American; American Trans Air; America West; Ansett; Avensa; Aviogenex; Britannia; British Airways; (CAAC); Caledonian; Canada 3000; Challenge Air Cargo; China Southern; Condor; Continental; Delta; (Eastern); El Al; Ethiopian; (Hispania); Iberia; Icelandair; Kenya; LTE International; LTU; LTU Sud; Mexican Air Force; Middle East Airlines; Monarch; Nationair; North American; Northwest; Nurnburger Flugdienst; (Odyssey); Petrolair Greece; Royal Air Maroc; Royal Brunei; Royal Nepal; Shanghai Airlines; (Singapore); Sterling; Transavia; TransBrasil; United; United Parcel Service; Xiamen Airlines; Zambia Airways.

Similar details for the 767 are:

Aer Lingus; Aero Maritime; AeroMexico; AeroPeru; Aerolineas Argentinas; Air Algerie; Air Aruba; Air Canada; Air China; Air Holland; Air Mauritius; Air New Zealand; Air Pacific; Air Seychelles; Air Tanzania; Air Zimbabwe; All Nippon; American; Ansett; Asiana; Avianca; Britannia; British Airways; (CAAC); Canadian; (China); Condor; Delta; Egyptair; El Al; Ethiopian; Evergreen International; E.V.A. Airways; Gulf Air; Japan Air Charter; Japan Air Lines; Kuwait; Lan-Chile; Lauda Air; Linhas Aereas de Mocambique; L.O.T.; LTU Sud; Malev; Martinair; Monarch; Olympic; (Piedmont); Qantas; Royal Brunei; S.A.S.; Spanair; TACA; TransBrasil; T.W.A.; United; US Air; Varig.

Acknowledgements

I would like to thank friends Iain Logan, Bob Henderson, Malcolm Gault and Ralf Braun for their assistance with this project. Unless otherwise credited all photographs were taken by the author on Kodachrome 64 film.

Below:

AER LINGUS

The Irish national airline Aer Lingus recently took delivery of two Boeing 767-300ERs on lease from Guinness Peat Aviation Leasing. These will primarily be utilised to supplement ageing Boeing 747s on the US routes. The airline also operates some 20 Boeing 737s of all four variants, and since the series -500s were taken on charge it ceased operating its four BAe 111s. A number of UK and European destinations are served from Dublin, Shannon and Cork, whilst Boston, Chicago and New York in the USA are served from both Dublin and Shannon. Subsidiary, Aer Lingus Commuter, undertakes most domestic and some UK routes using Fokker 50s and Shorts SD360s. Photographed approaching Heathrow on a route proving flight soon after delivery in April 1991 is Boeing 767-300ER EI-CAL. *Robbie Shaw*

Right:

AEROMARITIME

Aeromaritime was formed in 1966 as a charter operator, initially using aircraft leased from UTA. The airline is now a wholly-owned subsidiary of UTA and operates a modern fleet of Boeing aircraft. For European charters Boeing 737-300 and 737-400 series are used, whilst two Boeing 767-200ERs and two 767-300ERs, the latter leased from ILFC, are utilised for longer range services. Aeromaritime's affiliation with UTA is evident in this shot of Boeing 767-200ER F-GHGD at Orly. The UTA livery of a white fuselage with green doors and dark blue fin predominates, with the white Aeromaritime insignia superimposed on the blue. *John Sealy*

Left:
AIR ARUBA
Formed as recently as 1988 Air Aruba is based at Queen Beatrix International Airport, Aruba, in the Netherlands Antilles. Three NAMC YS-11s are used on services to Bonaire, Caracas, Curacao, Las Piedras and Maracaibo. The airline is partly owned by Air Holland who have a 20% stake. Air Aruba have also operated a leased Boeing 757 from Inter European which operated a daily service to Miami. This however has now been replaced by a Boeing 767. The now replaced Boeing 757 G-IEAB, was photographed in full Air Aruba markings departing a humid Miami in May 1990.
Robbie Shaw

Left:
AIR CANADA
When Air Canada has received the last Boeing 767 it has on order it will have a fleet comprising 10 series -200s and 20 series -200ERs. These are used on both internal and international routes. The 767ERs frequent many European destinations complementing the carrier's Boeing 747 Jumbos and Lockheed L1011 TriStars, although the latter are being retired. The airline's ageing fleet of DC-9s and Boeing 727s are in the process of being replaced by Airbus A320s, 38 of which have been ordered. These are the first non-American aircraft to be ordered by the airline since it operated Vickers Vanguards under its old guise – Trans Canada Airways. Looking immaculate in the summer evening sunshine is Boeing 767-200ER C-GDSP, climbing out of Toronto's Lester B. Pearson International Airport.
Robbie Shaw

AIR ALGERIE
Recent acquisitions by Air Algerie are three Boeing 767-300s,
which are used to complement four Airbus A310s on the
carrier's high density and long distance routes. Air Algerie
also operates a large fleet of Boeing 727s and 737s on routes
throughout Europe, North Africa and the Middle East. The
airline was formed in 1946 as CGTA, and assumed its present
title in 1953 after the take-over of Compagnie Air Transport.
As a former French colony the Algiers-Paris route is one of
the busiest in the company network, and the airline's A310s
and 767s are a regular sight at Orly airport. The airline's first
767, 7T-VJG, was photographed on final approach to the Paris
airport. *Ralf Braun*

Below:

AIR EUROPE

Until its demise in March 1991 through the financial problems of its parent company, International Leisure Group, Air Europe operated one of the most modern fleets of any airline. The carrier used Fokker 100s, Boeing 737s and 757s, with further examples of all three types on order, as well as McDonnell Douglas MD-11s. The company began charter operations in May 1979 from its Gatwick base to a variety of holiday destinations throughout Europe. Within a decade Air Europe had extended charter operations to include North and South America and the Caribbean using Boeing 757s, and built up a solid network of scheduled destinations within Europe. Its subsidiary, Air Europe Express, used Shorts SD330s and 360s on some 'short hop' European routes and on the few domestic services, such as those to the Channel Islands. The carrier's tentacles spread to include shares in Air Europa and Norway Airlines. Air Europe's main failing was that it expanded too quickly, and the loss of the airline was a severe blow to a market where at last there was a major competitor to some of Europe's 'big boys'. In a classic 757 pose, G-BKRM climbs steeply on take-off from Gatwick. *Robbie Shaw*

Below:

AIR EUROPA

Although the International Leisure Group was a shareholder in Air Europa, the demise of the former company has not affected the flying operations of this Spanish charter airline. The company operates inclusive tour charters to a number of destinations throughout Europe, as well as flights to North America, Mexico and the Dominican Republic. Air Europa has an identical livery to Air Europe, and operates similar equipment, Boeing 737s and 757s. Indeed there was some juggling between the fleets of the two airlines to meet their respective demands at different times of the year. Photographed about to depart from Zurich is a newly delivered 757 wearing the class B registration EC-669. *Robbie Shaw*

Right:

AIR HOLLAND

Based at Amsterdam's Schiphol airport, Air Holland was formed in 1985 to operate charter flights to Europe's favourite holiday destinations. Initial equipment comprised two Boeing 727s, although the airline soon selected the Boeing 757 and ultimately took delivery of five of these aircraft. Recently Air Holland has leased out some of its 757s to Sterling and Condor. In 1990 an agreement with Britannia Airways saw three 757s leased to the latter in exchange for two of Britannia's 767s. G-BRIF, a B767.200ER leased from Britannia Airways was photographed in full Air Holland livery on approach to Athens. *Robbie Shaw*

Below left:
AIR MAURITIUS
Since its formation in 1967 Air Mauritius has gradually expanded, and its aircraft can be seen at a number of European destinations including Frankfurt, Geneva, London, Munich, Paris, Rome and Zurich. Eastwards it has recently commenced services to Hong Kong – an extension of its Kuala Lumpur and Singapore route. The airline was formed in 1967 as a multi-national venture between the Mauritian Government, Air France, British Airways and later Air India. International services were inaugurated using a Boeing 707 leased from British Airways, though it eventually acquired two of its own. The international routes are now undertaken by two Boeing 747SP aircraft leased from South African Airways, and two Boeing 767-200ERs. Domestic services are undertaken by two ATR-42 and a Twin Otter. Seen on final approach to runway 27L at Heathrow at the end of a flight from Sir Seewoosagur Ramgoolam International airport is Boeing 767-200ER 3B-NAK.
Robbie Shaw

AIR SEYCHELLES

Air Seychelles is the national carrier of the small island nation. Formed in 1977 the airline commenced inter-island services for which Britten-Norman Islanders and DHC Twin Otters are presently used. International services commenced in 1985 with the acquisition of a leased A300 Airbus, and linked the capital Mahe with Frankfurt, London, Paris and Rome. Later Singapore was added to the route network. The Airbus has since been replaced by a single Boeing 767-200ER which is also leased. Air Seychelles has a colourful and imaginative livery, as illustrated on the company's 767, S7-AAS which is about to depart London's Gatwick airport as flight HM701. *Robbie Shaw*

AIR ZIMBABWE

One of the youngest international airlines is Air Zimbabwe, which was formed as Air Rhodesia in 1967. Domestic services are undertaken by three Boeing 737s and a BAe 146; the fleet of elderly Viscounts at last retired after giving many years of sterling service. The airline serves many destinations throughout the African continent, mainly using five Boeing 707s. The only European destinations served are Athens, Frankfurt, Larnaca and London. Until recently these were served by the 707s, however, Air Zimbabwe has acquired two Boeing 767-200ERs, and these are now used on the Frankfurt and London routes. Illustrated is Boeing 767 Z-WPE. *Boeing*

AIR 2000
A fledgling airline doing well is Manchester-based Air 2000 which formed as recently as 1987 to operate charter flights throughout Europe and to Mexico, North America and the Caribbean. The airline is a subsidiary of the Owners Abroad Group, and has a fleet of nine Boeing 757s which operate from three main bases at Gatwick, Glasgow and Manchester. The airline's 757s have distinctive stylised registrations in an effort to incorporate the title 2000, commencing with G-OOOA. The company's sixth aircraft, G-OOOH was photographed on approach to Gatwick in March 1991.
Robbie Shaw

ALL NIPPON AIRWAYS

All Nippon Airways (ANA) is Japan's largest carrier, which until 1986 operated only domestic services. In that year Government policy changed and approval to operate international schedules was given. The first of these was from Tokyo to Guam. This was quickly followed by services on the prestige routes to Los Angeles and Washington. More recently a number of European destinations have been added, including London. Boeing 747s are used on the long-haul international routes, with 747s specially designed for high density short-haul sectors used on many domestic routes.

Other domestic routes are flown by YS-11 turboprops, Boeing 737s and 767s. The latter type replaced the Boeing 727, and ANA is the second largest 767 operator after American Airlines. It currently has a total of 73 767s on order and, when deliveries have been completed, it will operate the largest fleet of the type. Current orders are for 50 767-200 series and 23 767-300s, over half of which have been delivered. Lining up on the runway at Osaka is Boeing 767-200 JA8239.
Robbie Shaw

18

Right:
**AMERICAN AIRLINES
(B757)**
Definitely in the 'mega-carrier' class is American Airlines. The Dallas/Fort Worth-based airline seems to go from strength to strength, and not beset by the financial problems of some of America's best known airlines. Over the past few years American has undergone a vast route expansion to a number of European destinations, and at the time of writing is in negotiation with Trans World Airlines to buy that carrier's London Heathrow routes. American already serves London Gatwick with Boeing 767s and DC-10s. Other points served in Britain are Glasgow and Manchester, with Stansted likely to be added in 1992. Internal services are operated by a vast fleet of Airbus A300s, Boeing 727/737/747/757/767s and McDonnell Douglas DC-9s and DC-10s. Its American Eagle feeder routes are undertaken by a variety of types. American is the largest operator of the 757, and currently has 91 Boeing 757 'Luxury Jets' on order. In a dazzling natural metal finish with patriotic cheatline Boeing 757 N621AM is seen on final approach to Washington National airport. *Robbie Shaw*

Left:

AMERICAN AIRLINES (B767)

American Airlines is presently the world's largest operator of
the Boeing 767, with 66 aircraft in three different variants on
order or in use: 13 series -200s; 17 -200ERs; and, 36 -300ERs.
The 767s which are given the name 'Luxury Liner' by
American are now being used to complement the DC-10s to
European destinations. The attractive American Airlines livery
comprises a natural metal fuselage with a red, white and blue
cheatline. The engines and tail fin are now painted light grey
with a red and white 'AA' superimposed on the fin. Taxying
for departure at Gatwick is Boeing 767-200ER N329AA.
Robbie Shaw

Above:

ANSETT

Established since 1936 Ansett Airlines operates an extensive
network throughout Australia. Apart from some Boeing 727s,
Ansett has one of the most modern fleets of any airline and
operates Airbus A320s, Boeing 737-300s and Boeing
767-200s. The airline is now known as Ansett Australia, and
has a number of subsidiary companies, such as Ansett
Express, Ansett New Zealand, Ansett NT and Ansett WA
which operate regional services. Illustrated is VH-RMG, one of
Ansett's five Boeing 767s. *Malcolm Gault*

ANSETT AUSTRALIA
With the name change to Ansett Australia the airline has introduced a new colour scheme. The all white fuselage remains unchanged, however the whole fin is now encompassed by a stylised Australian flag complete with Union Flag at the top of the fin. Boeing 767-200 VH-RMH is the aircraft featuring the new scheme in this photograph.
Malcolm Gault

Left:
ASIANA
A veritable newcomer, yet one which is doing exceedingly well, is Asiana. This independent South Korean airline, formed as recently as 1988, operated its first service in the December of that year. Initially charter services were undertaken prior to approval for the airline to operate on domestic routes in competition with the flag carrier, Korean Air. A fleet of 10 brand new Boeing 737-400s have been acquired on lease from GPA, and barely a year after commencing operations Asiana inaugurated its first international services to Tokyo and Nagoya. The airline is set for further expansion in South East Asia, and is planning to operate to both Europe and the USA. Two Boeing 767-300ERs have now been delivered whilst four 747-400s are on order. The first of the airline's 767s, HL7263 is illustrated.
Boeing

22

Above right:
BRITISH AIRWAYS (B757)
Rolls-Royce powered
Boeing 757 G-BIKX
***Warwick Castle* seconds**
from touchdown on
Heathrow's runway 27L.
Robbie Shaw

Below right:
British Airways 757s are
named after British castles.
Aircraft G-BIKW has been
allocated *Belvoir Castle*,
and is seen as it rotates
from the runway at
Glasgow's Abbotsinch
airport. *Robbie Shaw*

BRITISH AIRWAYS (B767)
Currently being delivered to British Airways are 22 Boeing
767-300 series aircraft, for use on high density routes on the
airline's European network. At the time of writing 13 of these
aircraft had been delivered, and were first introduced on the
Paris route. The airline is naming these aircraft after European
cities, and the first aircraft to be accepted, G-BNWA, is named
City of Brussels. *Robbie Shaw*

BRITANNIA AIRWAYS
A well established charter operator and Boeing customer is Luton-based Britannia Airways. The airline commenced operations in 1961 as Euravia using Lockheed Constellations, re-equipping with Bristol Britannias in 1964 and, at the same time, adopted its current title. The airline is a wholly-owned subsidiary of Thomson Holidays, and currently has a large charter network worldwide, including the Americas and Australasia. In the late 1980s Britannia commenced scheduled services to a number of popular holiday destinations, most of which have since been discontinued, though a Luton-Belfast service is still operated with high load factors. Britannia operates more international services to Orlando, Florida, than any other airline, it currently operates over 30 flights a week. The airline has some 40 aircraft on its inventory, mostly Boeing 737s, but also nine Boeing 767s, both -200 and -200ER variants. It also has three Boeing 757s leased from Air Holland until the six it has on order have been delivered. Lining up for take-off from Gatwick is 767-200 G-BKVZ *Sir Winston Churchill*. *Robbie Shaw*

CALEDONIAN AIRWAYS

Caledonian Airways is a famous name in the aviation world, although the present company is a subsidiary of British Airways, and operates exclusively in the charter market. The airline commenced operations in April 1988, taking over the operations of British Airtours. The bulk of its operations are to European destinations, though destinations in the USA and the Caribbean are also served. From its Gatwick base, Caledonian operates Boeing 757s and Lockheed L1011 TriStars, all of which are adorned with a yellow lion rampant on the fin. The number of aircraft on the Caledonian inventory fluctuates somewhat throughout the year with the interchanging of aircraft with British Airways. Seen at Geneva during the busy ski holiday season is Boeing 757 G-BPEC *Loch Katrine*. *Robbie Shaw*

CANADIAN AIRLINES INTERNATIONAL

The result of a merger between Canadian Pacific and Pacific Western, two of Canada's largest independent carriers, was Canadian Airlines International. More recently the airline has taken over Wardair, and that company's Airbus A310s and international routes, including the successful London Gatwick service. Canadian Airlines International now provides serious competition to the national carrier, Air Canada. The important domestic network is served by a large fleet of Boeing 737s, augmented by 767s. The 767s are also used on international routes alongside McDonnell Douglas DC-10s, whilst six Boeing 747-400s are on order. A number of A-320s are being delivered. As well as Europe, the comprehensive worldwide network includes destinations in Asia, Australasia and South America. The airline's Boeing 767 fleet comprises 12 of the -300ER variants with a further two on order. Climbing out of Toronto is Boeing 767-300ER C-FCAB. *Robbie Shaw*

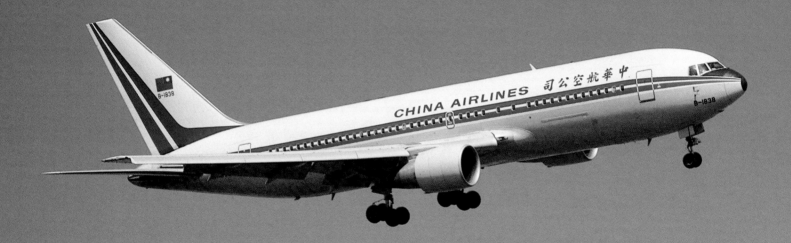

CHINA AIRLINES

A strong supporter of Boeing products is Taiwan's China Airlines. The carrier commenced operations in 1962 with a piston-engined fleet of C-46s, DC-3s and DC-4s. The first jets were introduced in 1967 with the acquisition of Boeing 727s, soon to be followed by 707s. The 727s have since been handed over to the air force, and the 707s sold. Domestic services are now undertaken by three Boeing 737s and intercontinental services by variants of the 747, including the long range 747SP. Two Boeing 767-200s and four Airbus A-300s were taken on charge for the fast expanding regional services throughout Asia, including the very busy Taipei-Hong Kong route. The Boeing product however have since been disposed of in favour of more A300s, a type which has proved popular with many airlines in the region. Turning finals for runway 13 at Hong Kong's Kai Tak airport is Boeing 767-200 B-1838. *Robbie Shaw*

CAAC – CHINA SOUTHERN

Another strong supporter of Boeing products is the national airline of the 'other' China, the People's Republic. Until recently the airline was known as CAAC – Civil Aviation Administration of China. However liberalisation has meant a move to regional airlines, and CAAC has been split up. Airlines with 'imaginative' geographical names like China Eastern, China Southern, etc now operate throughout the country, though it will be some time before all the former CAAC aircraft are painted in the livery of these newly formed airlines. The 10 Boeing 757s ordered by CAAC are now operated from Guangzhou (Canton) by China Southern, though one aircraft has been lost in a well publicised incident on 2 October 1990. A brand new 757 which had only been delivered weeks earlier was destroyed at Guangzhou airport when a Boeing 737 inbound with a hijacker on board crashed into the 757 which was at the holding point. The first 757 to be delivered to CAAC was B-2801, and was photographed soon after delivery on a service to Hong Kong. *Robbie Shaw*

CAAC – AIR CHINA
Since CAAC has split Air China operates international services from Beijing (Peking), including services to London Gatwick airport using Boeing 747s. Air China still operates the five Boeing 707s, as well as 737s and 767s. Of the latter, six -200ER variants are used, primarily on regional routes throughout Asia. Illustrated at Hong Kong's Kai Tak airport in full CAAC livery is B-2552, the second of the six 767s to be delivered to the airline. *Robbie Shaw*

CONDOR
Condor Flugdienst is the well known charter subsidiary of Lufthansa and operates flights to popular holiday destinations throughout Europe, and to the U.S.A., Asia and North Africa. The Boeing 727s and 737s it operates are in the process of being handed over to Sudflug, a new Lufthansa subsidiary. Two McDonnell Douglas DC-10s are used on long-haul routes, with Airbus A310s being utilised on the European sectors. The airline also has 11 Boeing 757s, including aircraft on lease from Air Holland and Monarch, with a further nine aircraft on order. Photographed on the runway at Stuttgart is Boeing 757 **D-ABNC.** *Ralf Braun*

Above:

DELTA AIRLINES (B757)

Atlanta-based Delta Airlines is another of America's megacarriers with a fleet of almost 400 aircraft, 129 of which are Boeing 727s. The airline concentrates on services within North America but, in recent years, has started flying to Dublin, Frankfurt, Hamburg, London, Munich, Paris and Stuttgart. New routes to Asia have seen the airline serving Seoul, Taipei and Tokyo. Most international routes are operated by Lockheed L1011 TriStars, supported by Boeing

767-300ERs. For the domestic routes the elderly Boeing 727s and Douglas DC-9s are being replaced by Boeing 757s and MD-88s, with 84 of the former on order, almost all of which have been delivered. This means Delta is the second largest operator of the type behind American Airlines. Photographed about to land at Washington National airport is 757 N612DL.
Robbie Shaw

DELTA AIRLINES (B767)
**Three variants of the Boeing 767 are operated by Delta. The
-200 and -300 series are used within North America, whilst
the -300ER extended range version is used on European
routes. Deliveries of 15 each of the -200 and -300 have been
completed, and most of the 19 767-300ERs are now in
service. Boeing 767-300ER N171DN was photographed at
Munich.** *Ralf Braun*

EASTERN AIRLINES
Eastern Airlines ceased operations in January 1991 due to
severe financial problems. A sad end to one of America's long
established carriers which was formed as long ago as 1926.
Over the last few years Eastern sold off a number of its
aircraft and routes hoping to remain solvent, however a
lengthy strike and work to rule by many employees grounded
the airline for most of the latter part of 1989. Eastern has the
distinction of being the first airline to put the Boeing 757 into
service, and had taken delivery of 25 of these aircraft. When it
ceased operations the airline had no international routes, and
its 757s were a frequent sight at Washington National, where
N511EA was photographed taxiing for departure. *Robbie Shaw*

Below:
EGYPTAIR
One of the oldest airlines in the Middle East is Egyptair, though it has only been known by its present title since 1971. When formed at Cairo in 1932 it was known as Misr Airwork, then becoming Misrair and United Arab Airlines. When services to Europe commenced, British aircraft in the shape of Viscounts and Comet 4Cs were used, however during the honeymoon period with the USSR a number of Soviet types were acquired. These included Antonov AN-24s, Ilyushin IL-18s and IL-62s, and Tupolev TU-154s, though from Boeing a number of 707 and 737s were purchased. The Soviet equipment has since been disposed of in favour of an all Western fleet. Fokker F-27s and Boeing 737s predominate on domestic and some regional routes, with Airbus A-300s and Boeing 767s used on most international services, supported by two Boeing 747s on long-haul routes. Egyptair uses the extended range variants of the Boeing 767, with three -200ERs and two -300ERs on its inventory. One of the former, SU-GAH named *Nefertiti* was photographed taxiing to its stand at Frankfurt. *Ralf Braun*

Right:
EL AL
El Al, the Israeli national airline operates an all jet fleet of aircraft, all of which are Boeing products. Numerically the Boeing 747 is the most important aircraft; the airline has eight rather elderly -200 series and an ageing -100 series. The airline also still has a couple of Boeing 707s, one of which is used as a freighter, and two 737s used on internal services. The majority of European destinations are served by Boeing 757s and 767s, though the latter type also operates on some North American routes. Presently El Al has four 757s with another on order, and four 767s, two each of the 767-200 and 767-200ER variants. Illustrated is Boeing 757 4X-EBM decelerating after landing at Brussels. *Robbie Shaw*

Left:
ETHIOPIAN AIRLINES
Ethiopian Airlines is one of the few outside America which operates both the Boeing 757 and 767. Three 767-200ERs are used on routes to Europe, which include Athens, Berlin, Frankfurt, London, Moscow and Rome. As well as extensive services throughout Africa and the Middle East where the 767s are supported by elderly 727s, a service to Beijing is operated via Bombay. The airline also operates a 757 freighter, with a further four passenger variants on order. Outside the USA, Ethiopian and Zambia Airways are the only airlines to operate the all freighter variant of the 757. Sporting the colourful company livery, 767-200ER ET-AIE taxies to its stand at Frankfurt. *Ralf Braun*

Above:
GULF AIR
Gulf Air is the national carrier for the Arabian (Persian) Gulf States of Bahrain, Oman, Qatar and the United Arab Emirates. The airline was formed in 1950 as Gulf Aviation and, from its Bahrain base, commenced regional flights initially with an Anson, before taking delivery of a Devon and Herons. These were later followed by DC-3s and Fokker F-27s. The first jet selected was the BAC-111, followed by VC-10s leased from the then BOAC. Currently the airline uses Boeing 737s on its regional routes, with Lockheed TriStars and Boeing 767s on longer range routes to Europe and Hong Kong. Six 767-300ERs are in service with a further 12 on order. One of these, A40-GG was photographed on the runway at Heathrow. *Robbie Shaw*

ICELANDAIR

Icelandair, the Icelandic national carrier was formed in 1973 through a merger of Icelandair (Flugfelag Islands) and Loftleidir, and operates both international and domestic services. The latter are operated under the title Flugleidir from Reykjavik airport using Fokker F-27s, though Fokker 50s are on order as replacements. International services cannot be operated from Reykjavik airport due to its proximity to the city centre and inadequate runway length, and are operated 50km away at the NATO base at Keflavik where a new terminal building has been built. A modest but modern fleet of four Boeing 737-400s are used on services to Europe, whilst two Boeing 757s serve Baltimore, New York and Orlando, as well as supplementing the 737s on some European routes. Photographed during a turnround at Glasgow's Abbotsinch airport, in preparation to depart to Keflavik as flight FI435, is Boeing 757 TF-FIH named *Hafdis*.
Robbie Shaw

JAPAN AIR LINES
Japan Air Lines has the largest fleet of Boeing 747s in the world, and also operates the 767, but in more modest numbers. Three 767-200s were acquired initially and used on the Hong Kong-Singapore-Bangkok run. Subsequently, 13 767-300s with a larger capacity were received. These are used on domestic and regional services, including the Naha-Hong Kong route where they replaced the long serving DC-8s. In the airline's old colour scheme, Boeing 767-300 JA8236 is pictured at Nagoya Airport in April 1990. *Robbie Shaw*

Left:
**LTE INTERNATIONAL
AIRWAYS**
**LTE International Airways is
a Spanish charter operator
which was formed in 1987.
The airline is 25% owned by
the German carrier LTU,
and from its Palma base
carries German
holidaymakers to the
Spanish resorts. The airline
also operates on behalf of
Spanish holiday companies
to destinations further
afield, such as Mombasa in
Kenya. LTE stands for
Lufttransport Espana, and
the airline fleet comprises
four Boeing 757s, one of
which, EC-ENQ was
photographed about to
leave Frankfurt for Palma.**
Ralf Braun

KENYA AIRWAYS

The Boeing 757 is a fairly recent acquisition by Kenya Airways, and is used on some European routes where it supplements the Airbus A-310s. A further two aircraft are on order and will presumably replace the two Boeing 707s and single 720 still used by the airline to regional destinations such as Addis Ababa, Dar-Es-Salaam, Entebbe, Lilongwe and Lusaka. The 707s are also used on the busy Nairobi-Mombasa service alongside Fokker 50s, the latter also being used on the Malindi and Kisumu routes. Photographed on approach to Zurich's Kloten airport is Boeing 757 5Y-BGI named *Jamhuri Star*. *Ralf Braun*

KUWAIT AIRWAYS
Now that the Gulf War is over, Kuwait Airways is in the process of trying to re-establish operations, which will not be easy as much of the infrastructure and ground equipment was destroyed or stolen by the invading Iraqis. The airline is one of those which operates both the Airbus A-300 and A-310 as well as the Boeing 767. Three of the latter, all series -200ERs, are in service whilst there are eight of the Airbus products. The company's 767s can be seen at London, alongside the 747s which are used on the trans-Atlantic run. Photographed at Bangkok during a long stop-over is Boeing 767-200ER 9K-AIA named *Alriggah*. *Robbie Shaw*

Above right:

LAN CHILE

With the exception of the British Aerospace 146, Lan Chile operates an all Boeing fleet. A few elderly 707s are still in use, one of which is a freighter, whilst a small number of 737s and five 767s, all of which are leased, make up the airline inventory. In 1986 Lan Chile carried out the first crossing of the South Atlantic by a twin-jet aircraft on a scheduled service when a 767 flew from Rio de Janeiro to Madrid, the only European destination served by the Chilean flag carrier. The only other destinations outside South America are Miami and New York. All Lan Chile's 767s are the extended range variant; three -200ERs and two -300ERs. One of the former, CC-CJU was photographed on the runway at **Miami.** *Robbie Shaw*

Below right:

LTU SUD INTERNATIONAL AIRWAYS

LTU Sud International Airways is a sister company to the well known Dusseldorf-based LTU. The airline was known as Lufttransport Sud (LTS) until it changed to its present title in 1988. From its Munich base it operates charter flights to the popular holiday resorts around the Mediterranean. Using a fleet of long range Boeing 757s and 767s the airline has frequent flights to holiday destinations in Asia, the Caribbean, Indian Ocean and South America. The airline has three Boeing 767-300ERs and seven Boeing 757s. One of the latter, D-AMUW was photographed on take-off from **Munich.** *Ralf Braun*

MARTINAIR
Martinair Holland which was formed as a charter airline in 1954 is now a well established carrier which also has scheduled services to North America. The airline has a varied fleet which includes A310s, DC-10s, Boeing 747s and 767s. The 767s, of which it has two series -300ERs with a further four on order, carry out the bulk of the scheduled services. Martinair is also involved in cargo charters, and its aircraft can be seen in almost every corner of the globe. Boeing 767-300ER PH-MCG is seen on a regular service to Toronto.
Robbie Shaw

MONARCH AIRLINES

Well known in the holiday charter market is Luton-based Monarch Airlines. The company was formed in 1967, initially using Bristol Britannias and Boeing 720s, to carry customers for its parent company, Cosmos. In the past few years Monarch has inaugurated scheduled services from Luton to several popular holiday destinations, including Alicante, Larnaca, Malaga, Malta, Menorca, Paphos and Tenerife. Monarch operates a predominantly Boeing fleet, using 737s and 757s, and has two 767s on order. Two Airbus A300s are presently leased out to the Australian airline Compass, though a further four are on order. In addition to serving the popular holiday resorts around the Mediterranean, long-haul flights are operated to the Americas and Far East. Monarch currently has nine Boeing 757s, one of which, G-MONB is pictured about to touchdown at its Luton base. *Robbie Shaw*

NATIONAIR

Nationair was formed in late 1984 to operate charter services, primarily to Europe, but also to winter holiday resorts in Mexico and the Caribbean. Initial equipment comprised McDonnell Douglas DC-8s, and further examples of these were acquired when Quebecair was taken over in 1986. More recently with the demise of Odyssey, that company's two Boeing 757s were acquired, whilst some ageing Boeing 747s were also taken on charge, including aircraft leased from Trans World Airlines. From its Montreal base Nationair now operates a scheduled service to Brussels, and is looking to further expansion in Europe. Boeing 757 C-GNXC was photographed at Toronto. *Bob Henderson*

NORTH AMERICAN AIRLINES
Formed as recently as January 1990, North American Airlines is a subsidiary of El Al Israeli Airlines and operates charter flights from its base at New York's John F. Kennedy International airport. At the time of writing the company operates a solitary Boeing 757 leased from the Ansett Group. The aircraft is appropriately registered N757NA, and was photographed about to depart from a rather wet Miami.
Robbie Shaw

NORTHWEST AIRLINES

Northwest Airlines is another of America's largest and oldest carriers. It was formed in 1934 and expansion took in a number of destinations throughout the Pacific and Far East, hence it was until recently known as Northwest Orient. The airline has since looked eastwards and serves a number of European destinations in the UK, Eire, Germany and Scandinavia. Northwest is currently in the process of a fleet modernisation programme, and the DC-9s, of which it has some 140, and Boeing 727s are being replaced by the Airbus A320, 100 of which are in the process of being delivered. Northwest was the launch customer for the Boeing 747-400, 16 of which have been ordered. When deliveries of the type have been completed Northwest will be the third largest operator of the Boeing 757, with 40 aircraft on order to supplement the 33 already in use. Illustrated is Boeing 757 N523US named *City of Dallas* about to land at Washington's National airport. *Robbie Shaw*

Below:

ODYSSEY INTERNATIONAL

An airline which had a very short lifespan was Odyssey International. The company was formed in mid-1988, and the first service flown in the November of that year. Three Boeing 757s and one 737 were acquired to operate charters from Toronto. During the winter months the emphasis was on conveying Canadian tourists to the warmer resorts such as Florida, the Bahamas and Mexico, whilst in the summer the bulk of operations were to Europe. The airline went into receivership and ceased operations in April 1990 – only 18 months after its inaugural service. Photographed at Toronto in March 1989, when the airline was relatively new, is one of the airline's three Boeing 757s, C-GAWB.
Bob Henderson

Right:

PIEDMONT AIRLINES

Piedmont Airlines was formed in mid 1940 at Winston-Salem, North Carolina. By the 1980s it had an extensive route network covering the eastern United States, with hubs at Baltimore, Charlotte and Dayton. The airline's fleet included over 40 Fokker F-28 Fellowships, along with large numbers of Boeing 727s and 737s. Boeing 767-200ERs were also acquired and used on the new Charlotte-London Gatwick route. Soon afterwards, in 1989, however the airline, along with its aircraft and routes was taken over by US Air, making that carrier one of the largest in the USA. Boeing 767-200ER N604P is about to taxi clear of its stand at Gatwick for the non-stop flight to Charlotte. *Robbie Shaw*

Right:
QANTAS
Australia's national carrier Qantas is rather unique in that it only operates two types of aircraft, Boeing 747s and 767s. Indeed until the acquisition of the latter type in the late 1980s only Jumbos were used. Qantas was formed in 1920 as Queensland and Northern Territory Aerial Services, whose initials form 'Qantas'. Shortly after World War 2 the airline commenced a Sydney-London service using Super Constellations. These were operated until replacement by Boeing 707s in 1959. In 1986 a new livery was introduced which has a large white kangaroo superimposed on the red fin. Qantas is now in the process of receiving the Boeing 747-400 series, one of which (on a special demonstration flight) flew London-Sydney non-stop. Qantas has seven Boeing 767-200ERs and nine -300ERs, with a further three of the latter on order. Named *City of Maitland* Boeing 767-300ER VH-OGD was photographed on approach to Sydney's Kingsford-Smith airport. *Malcolm Gault*

Above:
POLSKIE LINIE LOTNICZE (LOT)
Polskie Linie Lotnicze (LOT) is the Polish national airline, and was formed in 1929. The company ceased operations for the duration of World War 2. After the cessation of hostilities services were recommenced, and from then until the recent purchase of Boeing 767s, operated only Soviet-built aircraft. Two Boeing 767-200ERs and a single -300ER have replaced Ilyushin IL-62s on many long range services, particularly those to Canada and the USA. Illustrated at Toronto is 767-300ER SP-LPA *Warszawa*. *Robbie Shaw*

Below left:
ROYAL AIR MAROC
The history of Morocco's national flag carrier, Royal Air Maroc, can be traced to 1953 when Air Atlas and Air Maroc merged. Initial operations were conducted using Junkers Ju-52s which were soon replaced by DC-3s. Like the national airline of many former French colonies the Caravelle was selected and entered service in 1960 on the Casablanca-Paris route. The airline's fleet today is predominantly Boeing orientated, with 737s and 727s on regional and European routes. A couple of elderly 707s still soldier on whilst two 747 Jumbos are used on the few long-haul routes. Recent acquisitions include two Boeing 757s, whilst further 737s, of both the -400 and -500 series, are on order. Photographed heading inbound to Heathrow is Boeing 757 CN-RMT.
Robbie Shaw

Left:

ROYAL NEPAL AIRLINES
Owned by the Nepalese government, Royal Nepal Airlines is the national carrier of this small mountain kingdom. From its base at Kathmandu the airline uses BAe 748s and DHC Twin Otters on internal services, the latter being extremely vital and, in many cases, the only modern means of access to many of the remote and inaccessible locations. Three elderly Boeing 727s were used on the regional routes to India, Pakistan, Thailand, Singapore and Hong Kong, however some of these destinations are now served by Boeing 757s, of which the airline has two. The first of these was delivered in 1987 and immediately put to use on the Hong Kong run, whilst the second aircraft was the first 757 Combi to be handed over to a customer. Royal Nepal has now expanded operations to include Frankfurt and London. Photographed on one of its first services to Hong Kong is Boeing 757 9N-ACA *Karnali*.
Robbie Shaw

Above:

SCANDINAVIAN AIRLINES SYSTEM (SAS)
Scandinavian Airlines System (SAS) is the national carrier of Denmark, Norway and Sweden, and the registrations on its fleet of aircraft are split between those countries. Since its formation in 1946 SAS has been a long established operator of Douglas products. Douglas DC-4s inaugurated the first intercontinental service on the Stockholm-Copenhagen-New York route. Since then the airline has operated the DC-6, DC-7, DC-8, DC-9, DC-10 and McDonnell Douglas MD-80 series of aircraft. The only Boeing product operated was the 747, although due to lower than anticipated load factors they proved uneconomic and were disposed of in favour of more DC-10s. The airline has, however, recently purchased Boeing 767s, and these are primarily used on services to North America. Two series -200ERs and 10 -300ERs are in use, with a further four of the latter on order. Against a skyline dominated by dockside cranes, 767-300ER SE-DKO *Ingegard Viking* was photographed at Newark, New Jersey.
Robbie Shaw

Left:
ROYAL BRUNEI AIRLINES
Royal Brunei Airlines was formed in 1974, and the following year commenced services from the capital, Bandar Seri Begawan to regional Asian destinations. Boeing 737s were the airline's mainstay until the acquisition in 1986 of the first of three Boeing 757s, all of which are lavishly fitted inside. Since the 757s have been introduced the airline has commenced services to Europe, including a weekly service to London's Gatwick airport. Only one Boeing 737 remains on the airline's inventory, and a leased Boeing 767 is operated on behalf of the Brunei Royal Flight. Resplendent in its colourful livery, Royal Brunei's second Boeing 757, V8-RBB is seen at Hong Kong on a rare clear day. *Robbie Shaw*

SINGAPORE AIRLINES
Despite the size of the small island nation of Singapore, the national carrier Singapore Airlines has over 30 Boeing 747s, a number of which are the new series 747-400, dubbed 'Megatop' by the airline. The only other type used is the Airbus A310. Previous types operated include the Boeing 727, 757, Airbus A300 and DC-10. Four 757s were acquired for use on regional routes, but were disposed of within a few years. Seen at Singapore's Changi International airport is Boeing 757 9V-SGM. *Robbie Shaw*

TACA INTERNATIONAL AIRLINES
One of Latin America's long established carriers is
El Salvador's Taca International. The airline was formed in
1939 and, from its San Salvador base, currently operates to
five US destinations, as well as Belize, Costa Rica, Guatemala,
Honduras, Mexico, Nicaragua and Panama. The airline's all
Boeing fleet comprises six 737s and one 767, with a further
767 on order. The Boeing 767-200, N767TA is used to the
American destinations, including Miami where it was
photographed in May 1990. *Robbie Shaw*

TRANS BRASIL
Trans Brasil was formed in 1955 under the name Sadia using a DC-3 to carry fresh meat. The following year scheduled services were commenced, and in 1972 the airline adopted its current title. From its Brasilia base Trans Brasil uses an all Boeing jet fleet on services throughout the country, using modern Boeing 737 series -300 and -400s. Three elderly 707s are still in use mainly on charter and freight work, whilst three Boeing 767-200s are used on scheduled routes, including a new service to Orlando. Three long range 767-300ERs are on order. Displaying the airline's rainbow coloured fin logo is Boeing 767-200 PT-TAA. *Boeing*

Above:

TRANS WORLD AIRLINES (TWA)

America's Trans World Airlines (TWA), another of the country's aviation legends, is also suffering economic problems and has just sold off some of its routes from London Heathrow to American Airlines. It will then consolidate its UK services from Gatwick airport, from where it already operates to Baltimore and St Louis using Boeing 767s. These 767s, of which the airline has 10, along with some MD-82s and MD-83s are the only modern equipment in a somewhat ageing fleet. The bulk of the 747s are elderly series -100s, whilst its Boeing 727s and DC-9s are of a similar vintage. Pictured inbound to Gatwick is Boeing 767-200ER N607TW.

Robbie Shaw

UNITED AIRLINES
United Airlines is now one of America's largest carriers. In recent years United has expanded its route network to Europe and now operates worldwide. This long established carrier has flourished in the last five years, taking over Pan-American's Pacific routes and some of its aircraft, including Boeing 747SPs and Lockheed TriStars. More recently the ailing Pan-Am sold off its routes to London Heathrow and some internal German services to United, along with a few more 747s. United has to date received over half of the 54 Boeing 757s it ordered. One of these, N503UA, commences its take-off at Washington National Airport; the proximity of the city is evident from the Capitol building seen in the background.
Robbie Shaw

US AIR
One of the fastest growing carriers in the USA. in recent years is US Air, particularly as in 1989 it acquired Piedmont and its substantial fleet and route structure. The airline has only been known by its present title since 1979, having previously been Allegheny Airlines. Prior to the take-over of Piedmont other well known carriers, Lake Central, Mohawk and Pacific Southwest Airlines were also acquired, giving US Air a rather large and varied fleet. The airline still operates the six Boeing 767-200ERs it acquired from Piedmont on the Charlotte-London Gatwick route. US Air now has eight 767s on its inventory, with one more on order. Photographed on the runway at Gatwick is N645US about to depart to Charlotte as flight US1161. *Robbie Shaw*

Below:

VARIG
The Brazilian flag carrier Varig is a long established Boeing customer and currently operates variants of the 727, 737, 747 and 767. On some internal services ageing Lockheed Electras are still in use, whilst McDonnell Douglas DC-10s augment the 747s on international routes. Six MD-11s are on order and no doubt will replace the DC-10s. Varig has 10 extended-range Boeing 767s, six series -200ERs and four -300ERs. One of the former, PP-VNO was photographed on a scheduled flight to Miami, a route on which DC-10s and Boeing 747s are also used.